The Spiritual Mechanics of Love: Secrets They Don't Want You to Know about Understanding and Processing Emotions

Dan Desmarques

Published by 22 Lions Bookstore, 2019.

Copyright Page

The Spiritual Mechanics of Love: Secrets They Don't Want You to Know about Understanding and Processing Emotions

By Dan Desmarques

Copyright © Dan Desmarques, 2019 (1st Ed.). All Rights Reserved.

Published by 22 Lions Bookstore and Publishing House

About the Publisher

About the 22 Lions Bookstore:

www.22Lions.com

Facebook.com/22Lions

Twitter.com/22lionsbookshop

Instagram.com/22lionsbookshop

Pinterest.com/22lionsbookshop

Introduction

Many people wonder what makes relationships work or why they often don't work, and how we can make them work; but everyone knows, somehow, how to keep a relationship, either it lasts a few weeks, months or years; everyone knows, at the very least, some principles about love; and yet, because such principles don't apply in modern times and for most individuals, we still witness an increasing number of breakups and divorces, and this while gradually, more and more people, basically, keep on quitting putting the efforts to change themselves. On the other hand, what kind of efforts should people really be looking forwards to? Which studies truly help anyone in understanding what love is from a spiritual point of view? For as we barely started to comprehend what love is at a chemical level, a long way is needed to get the answers this book offers.

Now, the majority of the people do believe they are putting the right efforts in their relationships, most of which focusing on communication; and yet, they also admit that they don't feel understood by their partner. And although communication is indeed the basis of any relationship, there are many other factors interfering with it, reason why we are never satisfied with our results.

The whole world of energies around us and within us, manifests as well in our emotions, and that's why, sometimes, we also feel like we can't communicate with some persons. In order to do that effectively, we would have to understand this energy field; for there are spiritual laws and chemical principles that operate in the physical world too; and if we understand them, we can understand our relationships better.

Once we apprehend these principles well enough, and put them to use accordingly, they will feel natural to us, because, indeed, they are; and as you will see here, because these manifestations are occurring all the time, you will know too what to do in the right moment once noticing the information being displayed in your reality.

The Mechanics of the Subconscious Mind

People find each other or break apart because of one thing only: vision. They either share or don't the same vision. But a person who is not aware of himself or herself may not even know what type of vision he or she should have or build, and may not even know which ones are his or her own visions, and which ones are not.

As we are all telepaths (even though, because the mass majority is in such a state of transe, can't perceive or differentiate these dynamics, working within them, and all the time, inside their mind), we seem complex. And that is why so many people struggle to understand themselves, albeit this struggle is a delusional act of rebellion against our own nature as a collective, and which, once embraced, allows one to understand his true self.

Due to a very old tribalistic mindset that still remains present today in the majority, most people wrongly believe that this is accomplished through their group of friends (reason why they can't feel an identity when isolated but instead go into a depression), and in believing so, allow these friends to subconsciously dictate their identity.

You are never as lost as you allow yourself to be, by allowing others to tell you who you are, for that is how they think you are, and when you focus on that, you become subjugated to their thoughts in what regards everything occurring in your life.

We are, foremost, part of the collective we are emotionally attached to — individuals whose emotional mechanics affect our own. Within this collective, whatsoever you think of yourself, is nothing more than an absence of self-awareness dominated by the thoughts of others. And the less self-esteem one has, the more his group of peers is able to dictate his own views on the self and the world around him.

In other words, whenever family members or friends oppose your spouse, you are more likely to engage in quarrels; and yet, because so many people are emotionally co-dependent, they actually allow the group to dictate with whom they should be with; and they do this through emotional affiliation, i.e., for caring about what others think. And everyone cares, despite what they might say in public, for everyone wants to be approved by those they esteem. Both women and men tend to choose partners who increase the potential for this type of validation; and in their social validation, they find their own validation as individuals.

This is why cheating and abandonment represent the greatest threats to a relationship, for they invalidate all that — the group and the self. It would be like saying: "the type of guy you all think I should be with, was wrong for me"; and "because I did what you all wanted and expected from me, I was wrong too."

Nonetheless, we can't stop ourselves from doing that, for it is instilled into the mechanics of the collective. We may be more aware of it or not, but we are always choosing people who increase the survival potential of the human race into the future, and that set of values is often determined by the collective — cultural, social and family values.

This said, it is only normal that smart and rich women refuse dumb and poor men, for the opposite would be like a downgrading of the social potential already achieved. And what is normal for a woman, is to seek for a partner who increases her potential for survival; and she will go as high as possible in the social ladder to make sure she can get the best option available. Women have always been hypergamous and that's something natural to expect, as much as it is to expect men to get desperate for sex whenever finding themselves out of the optimal gene pool. That's where prostitution comes in, as a way to cash-out on our biological instincts driving our emotions wild.

Taking into consideration the reasons mentioned above, we can't possible equalize women's promiscuity with men's promiscuity, for no matter what society wants to believe, at a biological and psychologically level, whenever women are promiscuous, they are downgrading themselves. Men never become as mentally affected as women for being promiscuous, because, contrary to women, their gender value increases with the variety of sex they have. The more sex men have, the more self-esteem they get too, as sex increases their social validity. With women, the opposite happens, for you see, with every good man that abandons them after sex, they get the psychological impact of being devalued and invalidated. After all, that is a form of rejection. And they may want to think that this is not true, but their increasing depression ratio per number of non-marital sex partners in many researches conducted by famous universities proves my point — you can't beat biology with rationalizations. That's why biology will always defeat any feminist propaganda.

The Spiritual Implications of the Telegony Theory

The topic of promiscuity becomes more serious, and less open to social debate, when we realize that Aristotle's Telegony Theory can proven by science. In other words, women who don't cheat still give birth to the genes of their former sexual partners.

This study has been proven innumerable times on different animals and insects, including mammals, but it's such a controversial topic, completely against all the feminist movements out there, and above everything, the theory of evolution, in which scientists desperate want to believe, despite the increasing number of archeological findings systematically refuting it, that to give public credibility to such theory would certainly mean brining to an end any institution or scientist that even attempts it. This, among many other scientific truths, will never see the light of day, because the science of today is just another form of religion, manipulated by those in power to control the masses, but more effectively than any other religion of the past was ever able to do.

At a spiritual, biological and mental level, what does the theory of telegony really implies? It fundamentally validates many ancient religious and philosophical claims, while tellings us this: Every single person a woman has sex with, is incorporated into her own body of energy as well as her physical body, affecting her physical health, her mental health, her aura, her karma, her energy frequency and vibration, and also her own DNA. Even if she does not get pregnant with the men she has sex with, her offspring will carry their genes, and her body and mind will carry on their energy too.

In other words, every single man that a woman has sex with, becomes a part of her, forever and ever linked to her until the rest of her life. And so, when women think that they have the right to one night of sex with whoever they want, they should also not be ashamed to be labeled sluts and whores, because that's literally what they become. And they should not want to be anyones' wife either, because they lose any rights with their behavior; and here's why: They become a danger to the future life equilibrium of any man who wants to build a family, and they also downgrade the value of a society as a whole. In simplest terms, they must be identified, discriminated and segregated out of the normal spectrum of genetic options for any healthy man. As a matter of fact, such women tend to show the evidence of all this in many ways, despite what science may show us or not: They tend to have higher testosterone levels — like a man, be more aggressive and violent — like a man, show less interest in expressing emotions — like a man, and have less empathy towards children — like a man.

To put it simply, such women become more masculine due to all the masculine energy within them, absorbed from the men they slept with, and no matter how they appear to be physically, marrying them would be like marrying a transgender; for outside they may appear to be a woman, but inside themselves they are more of a man than probably any other man out there. You just need to consider all the blend of genes and energies within such women from many other men. The increasing trend of women behaving in masculine ways, especially in countries where female dominance over men is more widely accepted, is no coincidence when we compare it to the data of increasing promiscuity in society.

Promiscuous women are not only more masculine but also more prone to physical and mental illnesses, i.e., they represent the lowest level of the gene pool for men, even when their appearance deceives into thinking otherwise, because, somehow, we have been led to believe that feminine bodies are a symbol of purity and health. And so, feminist propaganda, while commonly targeting men, is actually destroying women. And the children of such women are never as loved as those of a mother who is more nurturing and feminine, more empathic and caring.

The Spiritual Implications of Our Values

Women are supposed to choose a partner, marry him, and procreate. Every man they sleep with, without going through all these steps, invalidates them as a woman. And so, no matter what people may say and believe, nothing will ever change the fact that men should never want promiscuous women for marriage. And they naturally don't, not even the most promiscuous among men; and this, because they instinctively know that a socially invalidated woman won't ever increase the potential survival of a species, and as much as socially invalidated men can't either.

Now, whatever this means, is open for debate, for it can indeed vary from person to person. Nevertheless, you will hardly find a woman who is desperate for companionship accepting a poor and sick man as a companion, as much as a man willing to have a spouse that is likely to carry sexual transmitted diseases or the offspring of another man. That is why single mothers struggle more to find a partner. And it is also for these reasons that men tend to prefer younger women, as the risk of promiscuity is often lower.

In both cases, most of them would rather die alone than accepting someone in the lowest stratum of society. And indeed, they need to feel very lonely and have a very low self-esteem to accept such individuals, as often is the case. This is also why, when you are in school, nobody lets you choose your classmates — you are supposed to grow into adulthood learning how to accept all the garbage of society into your life. And most people learn this lesson so well, that they become experts at justifying the most unacceptable behaviors and at appreciating the most disgusting people.

Whatsoever people may say to enable and accept social garbage back into the gene pool, they confirm these facts when seeking for themselves a type of validation that concurs with its opposite. This is why women keep describing me their ex-boyfriends as "decent, well-dressed, hard working, polite and wealthy" as if that said anything about the personality. Men, on the other hand, are more prone to the "she was beautiful" as if the princess, the whore and the witch, always looked totally different, as in the fairytales they got hypnotized with. And

I believe, such is the reason why so many people fall into the "angelic face" type of trap, for they are looking for social validation when assuming that a face says everything about a personality. And well, the more we need that validation, the more likely we are to repeat the same mistakes.

When the mistakes become too obvious to be explained, we fall into another trap in order to avoid introspection — "they are all the same". Both men and women say this in what regards one another, because in both cases they are seeking for social validation, rather than commitment based on an exchange of positive emotions and goals. You won't see successful couples, who struggle to continually improve themselves, saying such things. And such couples are usually rare, because they are composed by two persons who met by accident when focusing on the road to self-development.

People who seek social validation don't have time for self-development. They rather go clubbing and party than spend time at home reading and doing online courses, because a partner won't fall into their lap if they're at home. The more social validation you seek, the more social you will want to be, the less time alone you will want to spend, and the more attention you will put on the superficial aspects of other people, instead of their more intimate ones; and time will never allow you more than that, even if you want, anyway. In fact, most people that like to socialize in big gatherings have very little patience for profound topics or conversations about their personal life. That usually comes much later, in the form of "things you can't accept".

This increasing tendency explains why so many people claim to be happier in relationships where they "do things together". Because, this "doing things together", usually means being alone next to someone else, rather than evolving with that person.

The Spiritual Implications of Our Social Evolution

When people have a high level of emotional intelligence, and a strong character, they may resent the social pressure on them and isolate themselves. This isolation (which we witness a lot on empaths) does not necessarily represent an antagonism against the group or society as a whole, not as much as it represents an antagonism against the old self — old values. And this type of antagonism is necessary for one to grow, just like a lobster can't grow without leaving the old shell behind.

In the whole animal kingdom, different animals need to isolate themselves whenever going through growth, internal growth, as the external side of them is left behind. This is a natural process that animals go through when feeling discomfort. Only humans, with their social beliefs, tend to stop this process on a person. And they do it for the same reason why the one in distress does the opposite: It is as comfortable for family members and friends to avoid the discomfort of having to deal with the transformations on someone they know, forcing them to adjust to this new identity, while risking being rejected for not matching it, as it is uncomfortable for the one changing to avoid the comfort of not doing it.

This is why many fights we have with people are exteriorizations of inner fights within ourselves. We project and dramatize the emotions we feel within us, in order to understand them. We naturally do it as an instinctual mechanism to promote an understanding of our true nature — we materialize the abstract to make sense of it; we bring forth our inner world and project it into our physical and external world, to be able to feel alive, do deny our incongruences, to make sense of our nonsense, to justify our thoughts and emotions. We do this because we want to believe that there is an exterior motive to our feelings, and we do this because we can't accept the fact that we just might be insane — having emotions and thoughts coming to the surface without a rational explanation for their existence in present time.

No wonder the concept of "now" feels so new to most people, and meditation, as the act of breathing properly without thoughts, feels so extraordinary for the ones experimenting it for the first time. For they are never in present time, never truly awake, but within their mind, fantasizing answers and possibilities, that quite often relate to their emotional experiences of the past.

Only a very sane person would be able to make this distinction clearly — between the inner and outer world. But such sanity requires years of practice in being honest with oneself, while facing the social implications of it; and you can't expect an egotistical being to be able to do this. In fact, the more attractive and successful someone is, the more this person will tend to think of herself as normal.

Only sane people question their own behaviors, because they either feel empathy for others, or don't want other's reaction to be based on appearance but truth and reality.

The one without empathy cannot do that. She doesn't have experience in caring for what others think or feel, unless she depends on their approval to maintain her codependency, which in this case is rooted on fear.

We could assume that fear, as it is an emotion, could lead to the need to feel more empathy for others, to understand their emotions, but that's contrary to our survival instinct, i.e., the mechanics of survival are always prior to any other.

We can only assume that to be normal, for our emotions don't matter when we are dead. Our physical survival, in the form of a reputation, comes first to our thoughts and feelings, reason why so many people allow their values to be raped in the name of what is politically correct and socially acceptable or popular and admirable.

Now, to think that we may die for being discriminated is not a rational thing to do, and this, because we are dealing with primitive instincts encoded into our genes; but for thousands of years, rejection in a group quite literally meant death. On another hand, if you are discriminated at work and become the target of smear campaigns, the likelihood of being fired increases; and no job, equals no money, which equals no food and no rent for housing. And so, it is also normal that our survival instincts based on "what others think of us" remain until now and end up permeating all other dynamics of our life.

We only fear what can damage us, and we can't love what is against our survival; and so the insane mechanism begins, of studying others to make them believe what we want while ignoring any need for honesty — the formation of a mask hiding our real self is created. And the more constantly one does this, the more dishonest she becomes in order to survive in her social habitat, and also the more insane she gets.

We can't separate our social experiences from our personal ones, and so an emotional baggage is formed, interfering with other aspects of your existence.

Why People Dramatize Their Emotions

Whenever someone has emotional baggage, she will dramatize her emotions. And this behavior becomes so instinctual and irrational that such individuals often seem like they are under hypnosis when doing it. You look at their eyes, while they are dramatizing, and you realize that they are not really looking at you, but through you.

Emotional baggage is just another explanation for unsolved emotions, suppressed resentment, emotional traumas, and emotional immaturity. The more emotionally immature someone is, the more drama she will create. It is how she learns about herself. But, the more unloving and traumatic her childhood was, the more emotionally immature she will be as an adult. And that is how you see the past repeating itself in a new scenario, in an attempt to understand that same past when recreating it.

It doesn't have to be this way, but typically it is, because we tend to suppress our emotions when under stress and anxiety as a survival mechanism. Except that, in doing so, we also reprogram ourselves to keep the emotions suppressed, in order to avoid that same stress and turmoil in the future. It becomes a chronic behavior, to keep the past experiences (and their memories) suppressed from the conscious mind.

The lack of capacity to express emotions and process them, naturally makes one less loving — less capable of showing love, but also less capable of receiving and accepting love. One thing leads to another, which means this person will feel more loneliness, more unloved by the world, and more resentful, more incapable of loving someone. Then, to compensate for all this, she starts becoming more promiscuous. It's the only way she knows of getting quick love, in the form of attention. Except that this type of attention is delusional, based on sex only, and lasts merely for a short period of time. Besides, she also doesn't want it to last longer, and that is why she denies her own emotions, or dramatizes them whenever they come to the surface by exteriorizing a problem created to nullify them and keep then suppressed. And there we have, the emotional rollercoaster of so many people coming from broken homes — they want the love they fear, and they want the attention they resent; they want the validation that they themselves keep invalidating, by invalidating their partners and the partner's emotions, and they detach their body from their soul and heart every time they sleep with any stranger, while actually having sex with strangers to get that connection. Here is why these women feel such an emptiness inside themselves that they often contemplate suicide, and end up abusing alcohol and drugs to avoid such suicidal thoughts.

This emotional rollercoaster is felt within themselves and expressed outside of them. Inside themselves, because promiscuity is sought in order to produce the adrenaline that makes one feel alive, contradicting the void felt after every act, as it breaks apart the spirit, disconnecting soul, heart and mind; i.e., with every partner they sleep with, they feel more empty, and with an increasing feeling of emptiness, they seek more partners to compensate it. At one point, they need to block this negativity by hoarding as many attention givers as possible, and keep all potential sex-partners at sight to use whenever needed — whenever this void within them becomes unbearable.

This same emotional rollercoaster is expressed outside of them, whenever they consider having a serious relationship. Because as the rollercoaster consists of them wanting sex with someone they don't want to see anymore, getting the attention they can't emotionally process, they then want to be in relationships that they destroy on purpose, for the exact same reasons — emotional detachment. That is why they start every relationship with the prospect of ending it anytime soon. And quite often, they cheat on their partner to escape such prospect before it comes to fruition.

How this cycle manifests is quite interesting, for as they are afraid to be abandoned, they systemically put their relationship to the test, by insulting their partner in any way and form, by studying his weaknesses and pushing all the buttons they find, not excluding resorting to physical violence if needed; and then, once he starts showing signs that he might abandon them if they continue to do this, they move to the next person for fear of that same abandonment — the same fear that led them to continually test the boundaries of the relationship. The problem is, there is no end to this testing — it can last forever. That is why cheating is always the most natural scenario for such personalities.

Psychiatry labels such individuals with Narcissistic Personality Disorder, but any disorder can be deconstructed, as it is part of a specific process that shows itself in everyone. And so, I am explaining you all this, so that you may understand why promiscuity is increasing in the world and which spiritual implications it has on humanity. If you choose to call it NPD or anything else, is indeed your choice. One way or another, we need to address the problem as what it is — a spiritual disease, and the cause of toxic relationships.

Although it is not the purpose of this book to address demonic possession, quite often these individual are indeed possessed by demons and show all the signs of demonic possession. And this, because, promiscuity lowers the vibration level to such a degree that the soul becomes vulnerable to possession in many forms. Even mental illness is a resulting consequence of such lower vibration level, quite often followed by a vast array of physical diseases, among which the development of cysts and cancer are the most common. Among all the stories I came in contact with, it became obvious that these individuals tend to die at an early age.

How People Deny Their Spirituality

To protect their identity, reputation and ego, the most promiscuous say of themselves that they are liberated, independent and open-minded. Deep down, however, they fear never having a family of their own and the love of a spouse; and quite naturally, for the one falling victim to the drama caused by an emotional rollercoaster, will eventually exhaust himself, for being played around, and will most likely leave; but this only occurs when the one dramatizing is too stupid to make any conclusions about herself or himself. And unfortunately, the two things are indeed interrelated, for the more stupid one is, the more she will dramatize her own emotions on a partner, to try to understand herself while failing to do so during the process. The incapacity for self-awareness then leads to self-hatred, which is recycled back into more drama, in order to deny guilt, fault, responsibility and, overall, the pain of introspection.

These fights become more accentuated and permanent when the drama is fed by external sources, as it is often the case too, for the one who is not mature enough tends to be more codependent on the approval of others, whom, interestingly, tend to be as immature as she or he is. And so, here we find the mothers who were themselves victims of domestic abuse, and became emotionally codependent on their daughter, terrified of losing her to a husband that may take her further away from their life, offering what they call "mother's advice on relationships" and putting more toxicity in, for such mothers will forever be in complete denial to the fact that their daughter is insane — that fact would reflect back at them as being the cause (i.e., meaning that they are insane too); we also start finding jealous friends who are afraid to lose their drinking buddy; or a homossexual friend, who sees in his attractive female friend the perfect bait to get more men in bed; and, if this homosexual "friend" is actually "open-minded", or open to bisexuality, it wouldn't surprise much to notice in him a form of envy too, associated with a distorted form of attraction towards his female friends; He too will put poison in the relationship, making her believe that the boyfriend found is not "suitable", "a good match", "handsome enough", and so on. Whenever she starts complaining that her relationship is boring, such idea most certainly comes from the venomous snakelike mouth of her homosexual friend, the same one convincing her that bisexuality, smoking weed and promiscuity is cool, healthy, normal and completely acceptable. After all, why shouldn't he? That is his lifestyle and will always be.

To resume this explanation, the higher the level of immaturity, the higher the potential for codependency; the higher the codependency level, the higher the need for drama. Drama then increases the sense of guilt, and guilt leads to self-hatred, which is unbearable for someone already suffering with a very low self-esteem. The toxicity of friends and relatives, will increase the sense of guilt, therefore prompting the dramatization towards much higher levels. To get rid of this immense guilt, the guilty one then projects it unto others, accusing them of what she does: the self-hatred is recycled into hate towards the spouse and resentment on the relationship.

This whole time, the drama has been a projection of the self on another person, who reflects back at the first what she can't accept, and, therefore, projects back again, this time with more justifications; and, at one point, the justifications are so many, that the one dramatizing her emotions and systematically projecting them back, feels like she is going crazy; and she is — with every failed relationship, she sinks deeper into her own darkness.

How Emotional Baggage Is Reprojected

We could be tempted to think that the cycle of emotional abuse and drama ends with every relationship. It is certainly what these women and men want to believe, and what society, especially their friends, tell them to believe. But with every new relationship, they bring back the emotional baggage from the previous, dumping it all on the next partner, who now has to deal with his drama plus the drama of her previous relationships. And so, with every new relationship, her chances of succeeding keep decreasing.

With all that failure repertoire comes also more fear, which then leads to more tests and more insults, and more drama, and on and on; living with such individuals becomes literally claustrophobic — you feel like you are suffocating on their negativity. And you actually are — this phenomenon is also known as emotional vampirism.

Not being able to end these cycles, they cause what they fear the most throughout their life — loneliness.

I have seen this so many times, and studied these cycles so intensively, that I have no more doubts about everything described here. The reason why I know so much and so well about this topic, is also because I have studied it with many religions, after literally attracting to my life such type of women.

As an empath, an indigo, and a very spiritual and religious person, there is really no better target for them than me. What they think is love, is actually an obsession towards me — I have a huge reservoir of abundant good energy that they need in order to survive — literally survive. Meanwhile, compassion and empathy ends up being used against me too. That's how they trap their victims: by playing the victim themselves, and pretending to want help. And so, without wanting to disappoint you, I need to also tell you that knowing isn't enough to solve the problem. At some point, you will have to start giving ultimatums to them, which they won't follow, but instead take as a weapon: more reasons to have everyone else against you and on their side, proving that you, and not them, is the crazy one.

You will indeed seem like a lunatic for doing so, but for lack of better options, that is your only realistic option, if you want to end the drama in your life. You have to make her disconnect from her past and start a rehabilitation process with a religion; and it doesn't matter which one, as long as she is learning about respect, ethics and moral.

She will not accept the ultimatum: She won't stop talking to her venomous friends or reading their messages and replying them; she won't stop taking advice from her parents or reduce communications with her mother to once a month or less (and their mothers are usually on the phone with them almost every day, precisely because they are codependent); they won't stop abusing heavy drinks and being drunk often; they won't stop smoking drugs either; and so on. In other words, you have to let them go. Because they will never change or allow being changed. You will find yourself at war with everyone around her, and losing all the time. And you will be used as their scapegoat. In the end, you will still end up being cheated.

Once you are out of their life, they will quickly replace you with someone else, who might be inferior in looks, intelligence and social status. They need this person to block the invalidation process, the guilt and the good memories (which will trigger the sense of abandonment and failure), and that's why they can accept anyone. They will also destroy your reputation, to sustain this same validation: You will be known as the boyfriend who tried to control her life, by forcing her to stop talking to her "friends", and even her family members; the emotionally abusive boyfriend, that wanted her locked in the house, and never allowed her to go out alone with her "friends"; the jealous boyfriend who never trusted her; the boring boyfriend who doesn't get drunk with her and doesn't smoke drugs with her; the psychopathic boyfriend who tried to convince her to join a religion.

This last accusation is actually a delicacy to the most wicked around her, namely, her homosexual and bisexual friends, who very surely are atheists.

If you look at the society we have today, it won't be hard to imagine that any woman would support her claims, including her psychologist, her family will want her to find someone else, and she will never have to answer for any of her behaviors to anyone. The result, as she wants, is zero responsibility and zero accountability on her side. And yet, ironically, she was never able to take responsibly or accountability for anything to begin with.

The only thing that changed this whole time was your personality — you were emotionally attacked, energetically drained, poisoned by a bunch of vicious arrows, and dumped joyfully. You were used to dump the garbage of all these people and not just her. But don't take it personality, because, historically, humanity has always behaved like this. For thousands of years, these cycles have been repeating themselves.

How Love Changes Humanity

It is because humans fall in love, that they get a chance to rethink their values and reorient themselves towards their true self, which quite often represents their ideal self too. This relation, however, only becomes obvious much later, once the person finds the ideal self and notices that the transformations that occurred brought her towards what she always wanted but had no idea how to get.

The idea that our partner is responsible for it is delusional. He is only part of the same great mechanic of life as we are, being played by that same mechanic as we are. But it is through him, and the experiences he brings forth, that we are allowed to change. And so, we should never doubt the validity of a suffering that unveils layers of truth that we were not able to confront before, namely, the perception of what true love is, the understanding of what friendships should be, and the formation of a meaningful idea of family.

Obviously, put in this perspective, you can see why such awakening is so traumatic and refused by most people. But life never ceases pushing us towards it. That was the case, for example, of a girl I met, who grew up in a dysfunctional family, and was surrounded by people who enjoyed seeing her self-destroy herself in promiscuity, alcohol abuse and drug abuse. She could not handle these truths, but one day ended up in a hospital bed after nearly dying. During those weeks, I was the only person visiting her. I was also the only person who offered her books and tried to force her to stop drinking and stop consuming drugs. But she could not do it, and blamed me for stealing her happiness away. And yet, what she believed to be happiness, was a state of transe, a complete unawareness to truths she was not able to confront about herself and others. And because they are the majority, it was easier to label me as the villain.

As you can imagine, it is hard for her to deal with the fact that her family offers her alcohol to cause her to become an alcoholic like her father was; it is hard to believe her friends want her single and acting like a prostitute for the rest of her life, because if they are bissexual and promiscuous, she, by being very attractive, ends up representing bait for them to attract new sexual partners all the time; it is very painful for her accept the fact that she has been used and fooled into self-destroying herself by the same people she trusted the most. On the other hand, she is willing do die for them.

This example should be clear enough for you, in regarding the price that humans pay for their lack of consciousness. But a friend of mine, who is a psychologist, also put it well, when she told me that to be under the effect of the subconscious mind is a choice. It is indeed a choice, for you need to suppress that which you can't control, in order to live with it, even if kills you, as the opposite, a restart and a forced isolation, is too hard to handle.

The Connection Between Logic and Emotions

Most people are brainwashed by the media to believe in certain things, including social media, but also magazines, and even by their best friends and relatives; and that's how they lose the opportunity to get what they want — it passes them by and is never filtered by their spiritual senses.

They could believe that everything starts with a goal and clarify it in what regards themselves. But when they can't, their partner has to put extra efforts. And yet, talking about it, won't solve it. And this leads us to believe that lack of communication can indeed destroy a relationship; but excess of communication too, especially when such excess of communication is perceived as abuse and disrespect.

This said, how can we pass our vision of the future to another person? We can't necessarily do that, because there's an element here called freewill, meaning that the other also has the chance to accept or refuse what is given. And if the other person intends to control her partner, never will she accept a perspective that denies such control.

That's, quite frankly, the reason why so many people refuse to accept logical things — they want control. This need for emotional and psychological control is more prominent in women too, reason why they seem to not follow logic. Women do follow logic, or there wouldn't be so many women in college. They simply want something more than logic, reason why they refuse it with their partners; and that "something" they want is emotional and mental control over the other person. And the more their spouse tries to explain himself, the more control these women obtain.

It is known that whoever tries to explain himself is always in an inferior position when compared to the one who decides if the explanation is good enough or not. It would be like serving a plate of food over and over again, until the one eating is satisfied. And so, quite naturally, women also resent men who give them too many explanations of themselves, their thoughts and behaviors, as such men diminish themselves in the eyes of these women, they degrade their social worth; and that's why these same men often end up heartbroken and cheated.

The idea that nice guys aren't appreciated is quite undervalued, because in fact the truth is that women perceive value, naturally, in self-esteem, and a man that is subservient is not showing much of it. Only women who want to build a family tend to value such men, as in this case, such undervalue can be an asset, especially if the man has material wealth that this woman can access. And this brings us to the ideal "prince" of most women: The rich idiot that will give his whole kingdom for the cinderella, without anything in return, without even manners or respect. Somehow, the blend of fairytales with feminism, made most women believe that they are entitled to things that they don't even feel the need to work for to deserve, or men that fit a specific criteria, that quite frankly, degrades their own self-image. And the stronger is this concept in a woman, the less she will care for her physical appearance or even education.

That's the social paradigm we are witnessing today in many cases and around the world: seriously overvalued women looking for a scarce minority of men, that very typically are found only inside fairytales.

How People Fall in Love

Usually, people already have expectations in their mind before meeting their spouses, in the form of visions of things they believe can happen; and this set of beliefs is what shapes their future realities, therefore bringing to their life the correspondent person too. Now, because both partners are doing the same, they do indeed attract one another, but for different motives, different visions. Maybe one wants material wealth and the other wants a beautiful partner, and they both match one another in their wants. However, such relationships are always doomed to end, unless they share a vision that can be perceived as realistic for both, and that's, for example, the sharing of the same goal of wanting a family or a family business. And, obviously, many more other things can be added, like the need to travel, and so on. This said, what we find in society, is a connection or combination of visions; and we always feel more attracted towards those sharing the most similar to ours. This is where the "I have a good vibe near this person" comes from.

Most people are not aware of the meanings in the connections they establish with others because they lack both the understanding and spiritual perspective of such experiences.

What is known as the third eye, the perspective of God, vision of God, or Crown Chakra, the ultimate vision of reality, means understanding something that the majority of humanity can't see even within themselves, and it's also a higher consciousness that encompasses all others — it is empathy, and a truthful knowing, and a seeing at the same time; and yet, when you can make one person happy but that person can't make herself happy, you are proving to have an upper control over that person's reality too, exactly as what we see in adults raising children. That is an example of such higher perspective.

That's what you see also when someone is more mature than his or her partner. And this type of maturity tends to be confused with social quantifications, reason why many people, wrongly believe, that the more partners they have, the more mature they are. That is not true, because maturity comes from perspective and ability to understand paths beyond the majority or, at the very least, your own previous self. And so, when you are able to make a person happy more than this person can make herself happy, when you are able to guide another being towards the destination he or she wants for himself or herself, that is real maturity.

That is exactly what good parenthood also represents — it is the ability to raise your child up to his or her ideal self. Or do you think that a child will be able to understand that on her own? Whenever bad parents raise children, such individuals turn into stupid adults that are unable to even look at themselves and correct their conduct. They become the garbage of society, spreading their idiotic views on the world and bringing down everyone they encounter, destroying every single relationship they have. The more knowledge they have, the more stupid they become, because they can't detach their distorted values from the dumb things they perceive; they usually don't have sufficient analytical ability, discernment, or potential for self-analysis. Therefore, they end up associating themselves with the wrong people, making the wrong friends, following the wrong advice, and sleeping with the wrong partners.

Their world becomes a whole logic of stupidity very well organized and explained. And it always amazes me how much, people coming from broken homes, with broken lives and broken thinking patterns, have the most absurd theories on all types of justifications for what they do wrong, while assuming, in the same manner, that I have no idea of what I write about in my books, no matter how many people I help. Because, their stupidity and lack of consciousness, goes up to the level of assuming that they are so special, that what I write applies on thousands of people because such people are different than them; and even more interesting is when they consider my readers inferior in intelligence, because indeed you need to be a total moron to assume that a physician or a famous musician is inferior to some poor idiot with a minimum salary sleeping in a room in a shared house or with his parents at thirty and still not have a normal relationship or the ability to keep one.

How Are We Deceived

It's very easy for a child to get lost on TV commercials, social media, and feel sad for things he can't understand. The adult is not different. We are continually told what should make us happy or sad, because we have poor and weak personal values. And weak people are easily broken and changed to worse. You can't possibly think about building yourself as a mature person without self-control, and this self-control can't be faked or manipulated, but only built out of strong values and beliefs, which must come from solid knowledge. And I must say, the more stupidity I see in writers, the more I feel the need to keep writing, to compensate for the damage they do on society. There are many, truly many imbeciles, in all spectrums of life, sharing their arrogant and distorted views on the world, and destroying furthermore society.

Now, imagine this: A talkshow where five women share the same idiot view on relationships. What would you or anyone else assume? You would probably think: "There I have a majority in common agreement". Never do we question if that majority of women expressing their dumb ideas on society, represent eight billion; and much less do we reach the point of questioning how effective is their opinion. It's not like there is a researcher on this show that goes there and says: "Ok then, let us see, how many poor dumb idiots applied that nonsense and made their life worse or better" ...and come up with: "Imagine that! It's zero."

As a matter of fact, the state of our world can be easily resumed on the vast amount of attacks that a Psychologist named Jordan Peterson gets whenever he goes on television. Both men and women, from students to reporters, and in mass scale, attack this man for, imagine this, exposing research results on thousands of human beings. Because the stupid ideas of the majority matter more than the scientific facts, right?

The problem here is not as much on who this man is or what he says, but the fact that he represents science against mass stupidity. You can't really win in an argument against the stupid. Here we have someone saying "we did a well conducted scientific research and found this" being attacked by a reporter and TV presenters who say "I don't think that's acceptable". It reminds us of those who put McDonalds in court for becoming obese after eating their meals regularly. Shouldn't that be expectable?

My point is, we live in a world, in which people are so dumb that they now find justifiable having their idiotic ideas accepted. And then they wonder why their relationships don't work, and even visit psychologists to get answers in front of their nose. And I could give them a bunch of books with the answers, and continue my explanation on how spirituality affects relationships, but I can also assure you that you can't debate spiritual topics with someone who is not mentally sane.

Spirituality is not the alternative of the fools and the antisocial. And I wonder how it got infested with such degenerated souls. Because they compose the majority of the religions I encounter. Nowadays, if you go learn about christianity, hinduism, Islam or buddhism, it feels like being inside an asylum — nothing you hear will ever sound very logical to you, unless you are as crazy as those there. They then, to deny their own craziness, will tell you that all you need is faith, as if faith on stupidity brought any type of positive results to a person's life. And yet, we can also say that if you want to believe that, you will, as much as they attribute any natural phenomena or coincidence to the interference of God. Even their collapsed marriages are considered God's will for their own personal development; and that's nice, that's very religious, but not very sane, not effective, and not very spiritual either.

Why People Suffer with Depression

Many people were born in poor and emotional broken homes. And they grew sad, not knowing that this state wasn't natural. As adults, they struggle to accept happiness and enjoy a happy lifestyle. It feels unnatural to them at that point. And so, those who can do this, do have the power and insights to make such people happier. And it only makes sense that unhappy people always seek the company of happy people. The most insane and the most depressed will always seek the company of the most sane and joyful; and promiscuous individuals, although claiming to believe that they did nothing wrong, never want to be with partners that behave like they do, but instead individuals who are serious in their relationships.

The reason why everyone is doing this, is because, despite their social beliefs, they want to live a better life.

The contradiction between beliefs and needs, sometimes manifests itself in interesting ways. Because I tend to be perceived as negative by negative people. I complain so much about the state of the world, that sad people can't even be in my presence for too long, before either blasting into tears or shouting in disscontempt. But their attitude says more about them than about me.

This is the world we have now, in which a vast mass of people can't handle negative feelings anymore. They have lived with sadness for so long that they can't handle it. But also, quite often, this sadness is accentuated by their egotistical needs of wanting more all the time and not having it. They are the product of a spiritually empty world and are found more often in countries where the majority is spiritually empty as well — no knowledge, no empathy, no capacity to appreciate, and nothing to be grateful for. And to those who say that money doesn't define a culture, I must say that they have not traveled enough and seen the most miserable people in the most beautiful corners of Earth.

So many people are deceived by appearances that they tend to forget that most are nothing more than children in adult bodies. They go around thinking that they need to pretend to be an adult in front of other adults, and yet, forgetting that everyone else is doing the same, for the vast mass is composed of infantile adults. Most people go towards their 50s with a childlike mentality. And that's why we see the world like a big playground with everyone competing for the same toys, feeling jealous for the toys of the neighbor, trying to impress authority figures, and manifesting a tantrum whenever they can't get what they want. And because such people think like children, they often want to move out of their problems with the same mindset, i.e., by trying to build happiness as if it was a building block construction.

This can only occur whenever there is determinism parallel with free will, i.e., the capacity to think independently, make independent judgments and create independent goals. That requires maturity, or in other words, the capacity to think outside the social box that one identifies with.

How People Create Their Own Conflicts

The most interesting thing to notice in people who create conflicts is that they suffer from lack of self-awareness. And although they seem to struggle with this state of mind, it's not difficult to overcome it. And this, even if we can say that not all relationships are meant to last.

I could say that if someone reads all my books and follows my guidelines exactly as I explain, they will be successful in all areas of life and accomplish whatever they want. Those who do this, send me messages after only a couple of months, describing their amazing results and awesome new lifestyle. They thank me for the amazing relationship they have, the successful business, the new friendships, etc. But this is not something that the majority would do. The majority, as mentioned, are like little children, and you only have two ways of raising a child: You either have authority over the child and make her obey you against her will, with ultimatums, or you let her break her head in an accident and learn the lesson the hard way.

We want to think that adults are a bit better than that, but they're not. You can see a person repeating the same mistake again and again, during her entire life, and not even realizing the need for a change of perspective. They then seek an authority over them, once realizing that they can't have it over themselves. That's basically the surrendering to the childlike mentality, as if saying: I'm just a stupid child of thirty and have no idea how to behave by myself, therefore, someone else should tell me. And who do they seek for advice? Quite commonly that person is a psychologist or a psychiatrist, who, interestingly, very often has chosen that profession because he or she believed that in doing so, would be able to solve his or her own mental and emotional problems. Except that, quite often, they don't. And there you have, one big child teaching another big child, how to behave in a world of adults.

Things surely sound more realistic now for you, no? Because what kind of advice do you expect to receive on relationships when your own psychologist was raped by her father? We don't need to be so dramatic, but we should certainly consider the sanity of those who want to make others sane, as, from my own personal and direct observations, I have never met one single clinical psychologist or psychiatrist who is mentally sane. I do believe they exist, but I personally never met one. And the last time I dated a psychologist, I actually made her cry three times, simply because she asked me to tell her what I think of her. I did warn her that I may give her truths that she can't handle, but at the same time, I also assumed that, as a professional psychologist, I wouldn't be saying anything that she doesn't know already. And yet, apparently, I broke her into pieces with the truth she has been seeking all her life.

Obviously, I did not want to proceed into a serious relationship with such person, but this is just an example of how broken and delusional most people, and society as a whole, really is. I have actually had to report some psychologists on bad conduct, but these cases barely go anywhere, because society is built in such a way that any idiot can claim to have knowledge of how the mind works. However, these books wouldn't be selling so much if that was true. But that's a truth I can literally live with.

How to Make Any Relationship Work

When you share a vision with someone else and that person has the same vision as you, it is more likely that such relationship works and lasts. And yet, we need to be clear first about our own wants.

The easier vision that can be built towards the future, and that can be shared, is in raising a family. That's why this goal is so solid in joining two persons and creating long lasting marriages.

It's much harder to keep a marriage if there's no desire to raise children. Sure, dogs and cats can somehow fill the void, but in this case, the couple needs something else uniting them too in a stronger way. One of them, which comes also in a physical form, is sex. Good sex is clearly an indicator of a relationship that can last. If that wasn't the case, sexology wouldn't be seen in such high regard, and people wouldn't be having sex before marriage to decide if they want to be with someone or not. Now, if sex is all there is, this couple better invest a lot of their time and energy on it, in making sure that they are enjoying themselves, or they will easily get bored of one another, and seek something else. In some cases, this something else may come in the form of swinging, and for others in the adding of toys and more wild experiences. But it's a constant quest for more, if they can't find something else that makes them happy together. My point is, people start relationships by seeking something for their future, and the harder their communication is, the more they need this vision to make things last.

We are always in permanent change and we always meet the right person to help us do exactly that. But if one spouse is changing and the other isn't, we face an imbalance. This said, we only meet someone better whenever we are learning from our experiences and improving; when are more aware of what we really want.

Most people tend to focus on superficial things, like habits, conversation topics, cultural background, but the most important thing remains invisible even during communication, and that's our view on the world and the life we desire. Such is the case of knowledge, for example, which without persistence means nothing.

And so, if one possesses the knowledge and other has persistence, that's a good combination.

Now, regarding love, the same principle applies, for love is nothing without self-awareness. You will never go beyond passion unless you know yourself, whom to love and how to love. Whenever you love someone who has her center of focus on self-awareness that can work too.

Another interesting combination is aggression and kindness. If one spouse is too aggressive and the other is too kind, they end up balancing one another. The one who is kind will eventually feel safer and the aggressive one will at one point calm himself down. And so, the only way this combination can fail is if the aggression doesn't come naturally but as a survival instinct and need for control. It's only in these situations that you can turn a kind person into a bully, and then witness two persons battling one another like wild lions before finally breaking apart the relationship.

Aggression needs to be understood as energy, and not violence. You can be aggressive towards your work, the protection of your values and principles, but you shouldn't use such energy to impose yourself on another person.

On the opposite way you have kindness, which can't be used to oppress another being with need.

How to Manifest Love

You can't say that there is love without looking at mutual respect and empathy towards personal will. That's why many times people think that they are loving someone, and can't understand why their relationship isn't working. They fail to acknowledge these things, while looking at the wrong ones. Quite often, they are too obsessed with their own ego and needs.

The balance between two individuals is always alchemical, in a combination of heart, mind and desire. And we are all on this planet for specific reasons, for even if those reasons solve themselves in the material aspect of reality, they emerge from our spirit in its eternal quest to perfect itself.

Obviously, in less dense realities, other planets with higher approaches to life, we would understand ourselves through other more subtle ways; and so, we must address our problems on Earth according to our mental capacity, which is found in the interaction with the most dense aspects we experience, our strongest emotions and most visual demonstrations of self. Anything beyond that can be considered foolish play, reason why I tell psychologists that they are operating on nothing more than a toy store of human experiences. They see little with theories that can't address the fundamental nature of an eternal soul. To deny reincarnation or spirituality is always to deny what makes us who we really are. And it doesn't surprise me that so many psychologists tend to compensate this lack with spiritual matters, as much as it doesn't surprise me that they end up embracing the dumbest spiritual ideologies and practices.

I am not saying with these words that you have to accept reality on Earth as it is, but rather that you need to understand its dynamics in order to evolve to superior ones. And yet, once you understand life, you will also be able to appreciate it more. Once you can do this, you will also be able to confront your limitations and weaknesses in a different way. And such attitude will bring you more inner pace, for it is all about understanding how this balance works, inside of us, through us and with us. You are always limited by your reality and the laws of the planet, and you must operate within these limits.

The ultimate limitation is certainly death, but this death only operates on the mind and the personality. If people don't evolve fast enough between lives is only because they are too attached to the parts of themselves that are destined to end, and giving very little importance to the components that are eternal — consciousness, understanding, awareness, and empathy for others, for nature and for the planet. Even appreciation for life is eternal — we remember it clearly during our first years of life on a new body.

Our first years on a new body represent our first experiences with new perceptions, but we can always change them as adults, by using the same qualities we had during childhood, namely, imagination, good will, and faith that everything will always somehow work.

Our consciousness moves by will, and will emerges from desire; desire comes from visions, and those visions emerge from our imagination. When the desire and the vision are misaligned, we are misaligned too. But many decisions that we regret in our past, came from misalignments. To give you some examples, not many people know the difference between love and lust, a spiritual or a physical relationship, knowledge and wisdom, dreams and illusions, or visions and selfish desires, and that's why we have relationships, a family, and friends that reflect back at us what we are doing; and they can't hurt us as much as we hurt ourselves when not liking that reflection, i.e. what they do and say.

I am not saying that you must love other people to love yourself, but rather question your role in their life. Most people are simply there, in our personal world, to show us what we are doing. And whenever such reflection confuses you, you can always go back to the root of the problem, and ask yourself what your vision really is. You also have the right to ask your partner what her or his vision is, even though they may not be able to fully clarify it, and may even change it over time. Because, the goals of others can tell you a lot about your position and real meaning in their life. If you can see this picture of others clearly within your mind, it will also be easier to identify the best path for you in their reality, which will then allow you to better adjust your life accordingly. You may be surprised by what the other person tells you.

How to Attract Your Ideal Relationship

When I address the word vision, I may be talking about something very abstract, but it's also something very personal. Quite often, no matter if someone is projecting herself into the future or merely focusing on desires at the present, once in relationship, this concept of time vanishes, and both partners, either they are focusing in the same moment in time or not, end up finding each other in the same mental image. As an example, the vision for the present in one spouse, can be the purpose of raising children with abundance and having them as soon as possible; and the vision for the future of her spouse, can be found in a better career, more money, and a more state lifestyle, and he may also want this as soon as possible. Therefore, as you can see, they are both focusing on different time-frames of their projected relationship, but desiring the same thing from different angles too.

The future is always a present projected in time, and as much as the present of today is the result of the projected future of the past. You can actually self-analyze your results right now, in your life and in your relationship, by looking back in time, and repositioning yourself in the mindset of your previous identities, for you will see that you are exactly where you always wanted to be, either you are happy with it now or not.

Now, why would two persons who share common goals have so many quarrels? You see, the reason is also within the same solution. The real problem is that human beings are not able to expand their awareness to higher levels of compassion, not like what we would see in more advanced alien civilizations on other planets. And so, they are always fighting because they are actually always confused, jumping from one small perception into another. Quite few people on Earth are able to go beyond this mindset, and we typically find them among researchers, because these are the ones who, due to the requisites of their daily job, need to conduct researches beyond their limited and personal vision spectrum, and exercise the abandonment of their own ego and personal ideas.

Let me put this in another way for you: Until you can realize that each person can't be in more than one mindset at a time, you won't be able to realize that whenever you fight with that person, you are doing the exact same thing. Because, obviously, someone who is obsessed with his career may not work much on the house or pay attention to small details in his environment. His head is in the future all the time, and the more it is, the higher the likelihood of making that future come true. The same I could say about the one who wants to raise a family, and can't have a spouse around when needed, to shop for baby clothes and toys. Because, you see, the only way such relationships can ever work, or any relationship whatsoever, is if people are able to recognize their differences.

This topic has been quite widely misunderstood by a world obsessed with the genitals and a short sighted perspective of the meaning of life. Because respecting differences doesn't mean that your partner has to stay at home by himself whenever you feel like partying with your friends, or that he can do whatever he wants without discussing it with you first. When I talk about differences, I am talking precisely about the ones who justify the relationship, i.e., the differences that, when combined, make the relationship stronger and effective. Again, this brings me to the same topic explained above, related to the human incapacity to distance from the ego, to watch reality from different angles. Because, naturally, people always want to do things together in a relationship, but then complain that they can't get what they want, or that the spouse doesn't support them. As I said to one of my former girlfriends: "You can't possibly expect me to get richer, and allow you to quit your job, if every single week, I have to worry about how to spend the weekend together with you, where to party and what to do; In fact, I need to work so much more than a common man to reach my goals, that it's more likely that I won't do this, but instead leave you alone."

What do you expect a woman to do in this situation? We only need to apply the theory above to predict the right answer: She became frustrated, and bored, and started creating more fights; and eventually destroyed the relationship.

Now, she did try to come back to me many times; and why? Because she enjoyed the benefits of what I had and what I could offer. But you can't get the benefits without deserving them. That's why people have jobs. That's why the planet works with money.

How the Dynamics of the Planet Interfere in Your Life

Most people wrongly assume that the problem of the world is in a bad distribution of money or money itself. On the contrary, money is what keeps this world connected and operating as it is, for it would collapse in an instant if the masses where left up to their imbecile thoughts to manage life. That's basically what the dark age was in Europe — poverty, starvation, constant wars and crime everywhere. This said, how can I possibly reach my goals if satisfying a girlfriend that wishes to party every week? I cannot. And that's why instead, I was every single week, fighting with this girl. And the only reason why she didn't let me go, but kept chasing me back, was related to benefits. She was literally a gold digger, not matter how offensive the word seems or how much she denied it.

This brings me to another topic, related to the words that offend people. If you are interested only in benefits from a relationship, you are a selfish gold digger. There's no way to go around this. And if you have sex with strangers, you are a whore, either man-whore or woman-whore, and there's also no way to go around this. But it always amazes me the capacity of the human brain to justify anything. Because, no matter how much you go around justifying stupidity and foolishness, you are still being stupid and fool and paying a price for all that. And yes, even those who don't like money, need it and keep seeking it; as much as even those who don't believe in karma keep getting it back.

As I said to this girl: "If you want to quit your job, to be with me, you only have two options: Either you work for me in what I do, or you work for me in the house, by cleaning and cooking and washing dishes every day." I don't really care about what people think in what regards gender equality because the biological and financial aspect of life won't ever change no matter what people want or force unto their existence. If we want to achieve goals in life and matrimony, we need to respect the laws we operate it. You just can't fly a plane, no matter how much you want it, if you think you can do it while ignoring the laws of gravity. And I really wonder where did people got such an obsession with breaking the rules of life; for they would be better off jumping from a cliff and trying to defy their godly nature there. The rest of the world would appreciate it more.

When people seem very different and yet are very happy with their relationship, this appears to be a magical thing for the rest of the ignorant masses who assume that you need to look like your partner in everything to make it work. But I've just explained you where the magic comes from, and I also know that smart people usually understand this. Because they can think further ahead and beyond their own personal views.

Many times people enter their relationships precisely because they don't want to change. They start a relationship with a static idea of themselves. These are precisely the common cases, in which they seek a partner who looks like them. But seeking for someone who looks like you, is wanting to be yourself forever, which, in other words, means never wanting to change or evolve. Now, what does this attitude really say? Look at the people who enter your life with such attitude and notice what do they truly bring to your reality, and how are they improving your existence.

The changes in this case still occur, for you will grow more similar to one another. And so, you can expect yourself to start behaving like the person you have. If she is lazy, you get lazier; if he is aggressive, you become more aggressive; and so on. So you must look to the changes ahead and see if they match who you want to become. If you usually don't laugh much but your partner does, that's a good combination. But if you want to become a millionaire and your partner thinks that all rich people are evil, then you have a wall of problems ahead of you, growing thicker as you move forward.

This last example actually happened to me. It didn't take long before she started calling me evil. And so, we can say that, the more often she called me evil, the happier I should be with myself, for getting closer to my goals. On the other hand, she forced me to decide between love and money. And I obviously chose money, because love easily fades way in the hands of the immature.

Why Money is the Number One Cause of Divorce

You are more likely to find love with someone who appreciates work and wealth, and this because, as I said, we live in a material reality, and are karmically affected by it. People may deny this, but you need to look at their actions to make your conclusions.

The story described previously was about the same girl who wanted to be with me because of the benefits she was getting in having a richer man. In other words, she hates rich people but wants a rich lifestyle, so she insults her rich boyfriend. Are you following the logic here? There are only two outcomes at sight: In one, I get richer and am more insulted until I become poor; In the other, I become poorer to stop the insults and the fights between the two of us. In both scenarios, I get poorer, and she loses the benefits. In other words, I lose exactly what attracts her to me, and obviously, lose her too. One way or another, is a lose-lose situation. And that's why I said that the right choice is to follow money and let her go live her stupid life ideology with someone dumber than me.

There are things you really can't change in others, not matter how hard you try, because they are strongly wired to the memories and emotions of their childhood, their family values, cultural values, and so on. Their whole identity is wired to these things. So, naturally, the more you succeed in changing them, the more attacked you are by that same reality. And this is also what occurred to me when I was changing her towards what she wants and what I wanted too: Her friends, family and coworkers, all started attacking me, slandering me; and she took her side, reinforcing her own beliefs and values. Again, as I said, it was a lose-lose situation.

Now, let us imagine another situation, in which one person is good at planning, and the other is always lost. Who is in control of the relationship? Logic tells you that it is the one planning. But what if that's the husband, and his wife is a feminist, afraid to have a man telling her what to do all the time, as it affects her self-esteem, and she is afraid of what her female friends would think of her, and yada, yada, yada. Can you guess who will claim to be in control and even fight for it? She will. She will destroy the plans and create tantrums to get her control back. And what will she do with it? Absolutely nothing! Then, she will complain that the relationship is going nowhere. And yet, she doesn't allow it to go anywhere either.

This situation reminds me of a girl I dated once: She brought this attitude to the table when we were talking, claiming that she knows more about children than I do because she is a woman. I told her: "You want to compare being a woman without any experience in raising children with my degree in education and years of experience working with hundreds of children?"

Well, yes; this imbecile actually believed that, and even reinforced it: "Yes, but you are a man".

That was the last time she saw me. And yet, such women also think that they are very smart because someone told them that women are always smarter than men, whoever he is. And well, that's stupid. But stupid is as stupid does. And the idea that women are superior to men is a stupid ideology created by stupid people. The fact that many teach in colleges only shows how degrading society is and how low what we call higher education truly is. And I actually know this for a fact, because I was a college lecturer too. I felt like I was wasting my time there and would be using my time more wisely by writing more books.

You cannot fight strong ideologies, and these are the main reasons on what bring matrimonies to the ground. Because, as you see from the stories above, like little children, these people wanted to fight logic with ideology, even and including in situations where the ideology literally worked against them.

Maturing with a relationship then becomes very obvious for those who can see it: It is about growing beyond your ideologies and personal views towards what is beneficial and matches your desired outcome.

Money isn't really the number one cause of divorce, but stubbornness rooted on immaturity.

Why You Must Focus on Results

If you have any doubts on what was said above, focus on an even bigger vision of life — reality. Reality is energy but also facts. And results speak for themselves. If you apply the principles exposed in this book and see results, does it really matter how crazy others think you are? I have published more than 320 books, and most people still think I am crazy and stupid. What does this say about me? Nothing! But it says a lot about them. People also say I do't have the right to judge music, and yet I have been world Nr.1 in DJing and music production multiple times and without much effort. What does this say about me? Nothing! And about them? Everything! My students, when I was teaching in Universities, also used to tell me that I give advices that are contradictory with what all their other teachers, and even their parents, where saying, but those who followed my guidelines, are now all successful, while those who didn't, live miserable lives of quiet despair. What does the knowledge of other teachers and family members say about me? Nothing! And about them? Everything!

If you want to make sure that your spouse is tuned to your vision, you must connect his or her vision to reality — what is being applied at present time. Admiration is for this reason a strong motivator between two persons. They have to admire one another to appreciate each other, and this capacity is usually followed by mutual respect.

Even if you lower these qualities to their most simplistic application, you will still find them working, for the strongest seduction technique always comes from admiration: We want what we admire, either it is beauty, popularity, status, intelligence, personality, or anything else.

Surely, for these reasons, in some countries I am seen like a rock superstar, with girls always wanting to take pictures with me, while in others I'm like a bag of garbage with legs. It really depends on the social perceptions of the majority and what they value most. Now, what makes this explanation interesting, is that the two countries where intelligence is more attractive, are the United States and China. Europeans don't really value intelligence that much. So an intelligent person should never expect his or her spouse, if European, to appreciate them for what they know or read. Europeans are typically stupid to a great extent. And their projected visions are often based on acquisitions by copying or stealing from others. They want to associate themselves with who has success, but almost never read and learn enough to get to that level by themselves. And there wouldn't be so many freelancers in Europe right now, if they were not all working for North American Entrepreneurs. In fact, Europeans are so dumb and dependent on their system, that they often confuse the terms, and think that a freelancer is an entrepreneur himself. This is so true, that whenever I say that I don't need to work to make a living, and can still get paid while doing nothing, nobody can understand it. This idea is so very far from their level of consciousness, that they really can't believe it, no matter how smart they think they are. I said it to European doctors, scientists, psychologists, and even business owners, and they always look at me like I am insulting their intelligence. I am not, but they are just too stupid when compared to the rest of the world. That's all! And they shouldn't wonder why North Americans and Chinese are so rich. They should wonder instead why Europeans are not eating from trashcans like the many people of the Phillipines.

Most relationships can be resumed to what I just said. You can't break cultural values in a relationship, and quite often they are there from the start, waiting to be unleashed in either a good or bad way. How determined is your spouse in moving beyond his or her cultural background is what guarantees that cultural barriers may never truly be manifested as such. And yet, for this to happen, both must abandon the concept of nationalism and embrace the differences in what guarantees a better outcome in a relationship. Not all values must be embraced and not all ideas are to be kept. We must first look at what we want from life and the relationship we have, and only afterwards look at our past and the differences that imply a decision towards that vision.

About the Publisher

This book was published by the 22 Lions Bookstore.
For more books like this visit www.22Lions.com.
Join us on social media at:
Fb.com/22Lions;
Twitter.com/22lionsbookshop;
Instagram.com/22lionsbookshop;
Pinterest.com/22LionsBookshop.

www.ingramcontent.com/pod-product-compliance
Lightning Source LLC
Chambersburg PA
CBHW050449010526
44118CB00013B/1752